The Ultimate Air Fryer Recipe Book

Beginner Tips And Tricks To Make Your Meals Taste Fabulous

Joseph Biggs

Copyright © [2022] [Joseph Biggs]

All rights reserved

All rights for this book here presented belong exclusively to the author. Usage or reproduction of the text is forbidden and requires a clear consent of the author in case of expectations.

ISBN - 9798816915595

Table of Contents

Introduction 7
  What is an Air Fryer? 8
  What to Look For When Buying a New Air Fryer 10
  Looking After Your Air Fryer 11
  General Tips For Getting The Most Out of Your Air Fryer 13
  Air Fryer Breakfast Recipes 15
    Air Fryer French Toast 16
    Burgers For Breakfast 17
    Cheesy "Oven" Eggs 18
    Vegetable Hash Browns 19
    Bacon & Mozzarella Toast 20
    Egg & Ham Cups 21
    Scrambled Eggs With Cheese 22
    Cheesy Chorizo Frittata 23
    Swiss Cheese Breakfast Sandwich 24
    Spicy Breakfast Wrap 25
    Fruity Breakfast Muffins 26
    Stuffed Bell Peppers 27
    Homemade Breakfast Bagels 28
    Sweet Potato Hash 29
    Berry Pockets 30

  Air Fryer Lunch Recipes 31
    Peppery Chicken Wings 32
    Mediterranean Chicken Balls 33
    Breaded Chicken Tenders 34
    Popcorn Shrimp With a Kick 35
    Panky Calamari 36
    Lime Salmon Patties 37

Steak Bites 38
Beef & Courgette (Zucchini) Frittata 39
Lamb & Harissa Burgers 41
Swiss Cheese & Ham Sliders 42
Potato & Carrot Burgers 43
Italian Ravioli 44
Onion Dumplings 45
Italian Aubergine (Eggplant) Parmesan 46
Spicy Buffalo Wings 48

Air Fryer Dinner Recipes 49
Mushroom & Turkey Cutlets 50
Spicy Chicken Chimichangas 51
Furikake & Mayo Salmon 52
Breaded Fish Fillets With Ranch 53
Traditional Beef Wellington 54
Coconut & Ginger Beef 55
Classic Beef Satay 56
Mustard & Garlic Pork Tenderloin 57
Balsamic Pork Chops with Raspberry 58
Balsamic Gnocchi Caprese 59
Garlic & Citrus Cauliflower 60
Falafel Patties 62
Tikka Paneer 64
Creamy Mushroom Pasta 66
Garlic Buttermilk Chicken 67

Air Fryer Dessert Recipes 69
Key Lime Cupcakes 70
Chocolate & Vanilla Biscuits 71
Coconut Fried Bananas 72
Citrus & Chocolate Fondant 73
Chocolate Citrus Muffins 74
Classic Profiteroles 75

    New York Cheesecake 77
    Creamy Cherry Pies 79
    Chocolate Soufflé 80
    Decadent Chocolate Cake 81
    Strawberry "Pop-Tarts" 82
    Chocolate Eclairs 84
    Banana & Peanut Butter Bites 85
    Pistachio & Pecan Brownies 86
    Fruity Nutella Sandwich 87
    Peach Pies 88

Air Fryer Side Recipes 89
    Spicy Rice 90
    Avocado "Chips" 91
    Parmesan Asparagus 92
    Balsamic Brussels 93
    Corn on The Cob 94
    Herby Baby Potatoes 95
    Cheesy Shishito Peppers 96
    Mini Aubergine (Eggplant) Bites 97
    Cheesy Carrot Fries 98
    Spinach Stuffed Potatoes 99
    Citrus & Garlic Tofu 100
    Courgette (Zucchini) Gratin 101
    Salty Chickpeas 102
    Spicy Pickles 103
    BBQ Bacon Parcels 104

Conclusion 105

Disclaimer 108

EXCLUSIVE BONUS

40 Weight Loss Recipes

&

14 Days Meal Plan

Scan the QR-Code and receive the FREE download:

Introduction

An air fryer is one of those things that we're either given as a gift and don't quite know how to use, or we buy it full of good intentions and then forget about because we don't know what to do. Basically, it's a waste because air fryers are fantastic kitchen gadgets that can help you to create delicious foods, very quickly, and with that delicious crisp, zero-dripping-in-oil taste.

So, if you have an air fryer in your kitchen and you're confused as to how to even turn it on, or you've seen one in the sale and you're considering buying it, this book will answer your questions and help to inspire you along the way. After all, air fryers are created for a reason and that's because they're great!

We're not only going to give you the lowdown on air fryers and what to do with them, but we're going to inspire you to get started too! In these pages you'll find delicious recipes for breakfast, lunch, dinner, dessert, and sides too, all made in your trusty air fryer.

The truth is that an air fryer is very flexible. You can make so many things in it that you probably don't even realise. For instance, did you know that you can make desserts in your air fryer? It's true! You can also make your meals much healthier and much crisper, all thanks to the fact that you're not drenching your food in oil. You're literally frying in air!

But, because an air fryer is probably a totally new gadget to you, we need to start at the beginning. What exactly is an air fryer, what does it do, and how do you use it?

What is an Air Fryer?

Air fryers have been around for a long time but they're enjoying somewhat of a boom lately. That's probably because we're all focused on becoming healthier and an air fryer can help you to create meals in that healthy and clean way. All with minimal fuss too.

Basically, an air fryer is a kitchen appliance. You use it to cook your food but you cook with high temperature air, rather than resorting to oil. It's totally different from the old-fashioned deep fat fryer. That was not healthy and still isn't!

A deep fat fryer basically cooks your food in a large amount of fat/oil and you get crispy yet extremely unhealthy results. On the other hand, an air fryer doesn't use fat or oil, it just uses hot air to cook your food and therefore gives it that delicious crisp we all love.

If you've ever tried chips/fries cooked in an air fryer you'll never go back to the regular way. They're so much lighter, crisper, and just taste so much better. You're getting all of that without eating unhealthy oils that massively contribute to negative health impacts, such as high cholesterol, heart issues, and clogged arteries.

Air fryers use high impact convection methods to cook your food. Inside your fryer there is a heavy-duty fan that works to circulate air all around your food, making sure that it's totally cooked, evenly and properly. That means all the ingredients you place into your air fryer are cooked to perfection.

What you'll get in the end is a result that could easily have come from a restaurant yet you made it at home, far cheaper and with less stress.

Do you need to be experienced in cooking to use an air fryer? No! There are different models on the market and you should shop around for the best one to suit your needs. Some are more complicated and have more functions, but the basic air fryers on the market are ideal for beginners. There is nothing more complicated than placing the ingredients into the machine, following the instructions according to your particular model, and waiting for your food to cook. That's literally all there is to it.

Of course, the one downside of an air fryer is the cost. They don't come free, but you can find air fryers of a high quality that have a lower price tag; it's all about shopping around.

You might be wondering why you should bother splurging the cash when you can carry on with your usual cooking methods. That's a fair point, but there are some great benefits of purchasing and using an air fryer. Remember, this isn't something you should buy and then place in the back of your kitchen cupboard because you don't know how to use it - you need to get the most out of it!

- Air fryers are easy to use and are suitable for all ability levels
- Your food cooks evenly
- Faster cooking times compared to other cooking methods
- Less fat content, due to cooking in hot air, rather than oil and fat
- That famous light and crispy feel to your food
- Most air fryers are very easy to maintain and many can be cleaned in the dishwasher
- No strong smell of fat or oil in the air while you're cooking
- You can cook frozen foods very quickly
- Many newer air fryer models are designed to be energy efficient
- Allows you to cook many different meals easily and saves a lot of time during a working week
- Most newer models are compact and easy to store

What to Look For When Buying a New Air Fryer

You're not the only person to think about buying an air fryer for the first time, and that means many people are going to be wondering about what they should consider before splashing the cash. Even if you've owned an air fryer previously, the newer models are much sleeker and full of more features than before. That means you need to be up to date with what to look for before spending your money.

It's important to remember that not everything is suitable to cook in an air fryer, so that's something to bear in mind. You can't cook batters in your air fryer, but most other things can be cooked very easily in this flexible and versatile appliance. Also, unless you opt to buy a large volume air fryer (quite hard to find) then you're probably going to need to cook meals for many people in batches. If you have a large family and that's an issue for you, you'll need to think carefully about the time you spend cooking before deciding whether or not to buy an air fryer. For most people however, a regular air fryer will accommodate enough for a regular sized family.

So, what elements should you think about when purchasing an air fryer? The main things to bear in mind are:
- Budget
- Range of features you want
- Storage space
- Guarantee
- Model and brand name

Your budget is probably the most important thing to consider first. By looking around before making a decision you'll be able to find an air fryer that not only fits your budget but one that covers all your other requirement bases too. When you go for an air fryer with a larger capacity and one that has more in the way of features, you're going to end up paying more. That's just common sense. But, if you go for a regular sized, middle-range air fryer, you'll find a lot of choice and a range of prices to choose from.

You need to do a little careful thinking and identify the features that are most important to you. Most first time users aren't going to need a top of the range air fryer, but there may be specific things that you want, e.g., capacity. The only way to work this particular issue out is to do your homework and then use that when you go out shopping for your new appliance.

As for storage space, that will vary from person to person. As before, most air fryers these days are compact and quite easy to store, but larger capacity air fryers will obviously need somewhere specific to store them, unless you have a large countertop and you're going to use it often.

The final points of brand name and guarantee are also important. Make sure that you purchase an air fryer that has at least a year's guarantee. That way, if anything goes wrong initially, you can get it fixed. However, brand name doesn't always have to matter too much. As long as the air fryer is quality, and you can check reviews to give you important insights, then the brand name may only be something that gives you peace of mind and not necessarily a make or break part of your purchasing experience.

Looking After Your Air Fryer

Not only do you need to know how to use your air fryer, but you also need to know how to look after it properly. That way, you'll avoid any major problems and your costly appliance will last far longer.

Every air fryer has different instructions for use. We can't really give you information on that because it will vary wildly from model to model, and brand to brand. The best advice in that regard is to read the instruction booklet you get with your air fryer very carefully and follow that advice. That way, you know you're using it correctly and you're going to get years of use out of it.

However, you also need to know how to maintain and look after your air fryer. That's also very important.

When you look after your new purchase it will last the test of time and you'll find you experience less hiccups and glitches. There aren't too many things you need to know about this, but you do need to know how to clean it effectively and there are also a few troubleshooting tips you should learn too. That way, you'll know what to look for and how to fix any issues that do come your way. Much of the time, small issues can be fixed simply by changing how you use the appliance.

Cleaning your air fryer is the most important thing to learn about. Most air fryers can be cleaned in the dish washer but this does vary slightly from model to model, so check the instruction booklet before you load it into the dish washer for the first time! You will need to clean your appliance every time you use it, but when you consider the fact that you have to clean pots and pans when you use them, it makes sense!

Most modern appliances these days have parts that are easily removed and cleaned, which can then be put back in with ease. Gone are the days when air fryers were large, bulky machines that needed to be cleaned without being taken apart! However, do remember that the main appliance part of your air fryer is electric so don't put it in water.

Another point to remember when cleaning your air fryer is that there is a special coating on the inside that can easily be scratched if you use scouring pads or abrasive cloths. Use a soft cloth and you'll avoid this problem.

You should also store your air fryer somewhere dry. If you're keeping it on your countertop, make sure it's not sitting in a puddle of water as it's drying. Also, if you're keeping it in a cupboard, make sure you use it often to give it some air and to stop parts from becoming stiff. Of course, by the end of this book you'll be so inspired with what to make in your air fryer that it's always in use, so that shouldn't be an issue!

General Tips For Getting The Most Out of Your Air Fryer

While every air fryer will have a slightly different way to be used, there are some pretty general tips that all models work hand in hand with. These quick and easy tips will help you to maximise the potential of your air fryer and allow you to get the most out of it.

It's also important to remember that you're learning to use something for the first time and that means you should take your time. There may be the odd fail along the way but that's fine! You'll do it better next time. We know that air fryers are pretty easy to use these days, but sometimes we make mistakes when learning how to use a new appliance. Don't become disheartened if something doesn't work out the way you want it to immediately, just keep trying!

So, before we get onto the fun part of learning how to create delicious and healthy meals with your new air fryer, let's look at some general tips that will allow you to get started in a successful way.

- Even though you aren't cooking your food in oil, it's a good idea to very lightly coat your food with a small amount of oil before placing it inside the fryer. This will ensure that nothing sticks to the bottom of the air fryer. But, if you're cooking something that

already has a slightly oily exterior, e.g., meat, you don't need to worry about adding extra.
- Heat your fryer up a little before you're going to use it. When it's at the temperature you want it to be at, that's when you can put your food inside and start to cook. You'll get that perfect crunch by doing this and you'll avoid any potential for sogginess.
- Don't overcrowd the air fryer basket. If you find the need to do this, it's because you've not purchased an air fryer with a large enough capacity. In that case, you'll need to repurchase (costly - always do your homework first), or you'll need to cook your food in separate batches to get the desired outcome and to avoid causing technical problems with your appliance.
- For extra crunch, you could consider using a low fat cooking spray and giving the ingredients a very light spray halfway through cooking. This isn't a necessity, but it does help with crunchiness!
- Hot doesn't always mean crunchy. Different ingredients will crunch in different ways so make sure that you play around with temperature and find the happy medium. This will come over time - don't worry if it doesn't happen immediately.
- It's good practice to give your food a shake periodically, especially if you're cooking foods like chips/fries or even chicken wings. This will ensure they don't stick and will help to crisp all sides.

Now you know all the basics when it comes to air fryers. Whether you have one already or you're about to purchase one, you'll certainly be able to make some delicious foods with your new appliance. All you need to do is work out what you want to try first and then go for it.

Practice makes perfect!

Air Fryer Breakfast Recipes

Breakfast is the most important meal of the day but that doesn't mean you need to get the frying pan out and start frying everything in oil! Your air fryer has the ability to create some seriously delicious, not to mention healthy, recipes.

Let's check out some fantastic breakfast choices you can make in your new air fryer.

Air Fryer French Toast

Servings - 1
Calories - 302, protein - 3g, fat - 1g, carbs - 23g

Ingredients

- 5 slices of bread - sandwich bread works best
- 2 medium eggs
- 2 tbsp flour
- 3 tbsp white sugar
- 100ml/0.5 cups of milk
- 0.5 tsp vanilla extract
- 1 tsp ground cinnamon
- 0.5 tsp salt

Method

1. Preheat the air fryer to 220C/390F and place a piece of parchment paper inside
2. Cut each slice of bread into three equal pieces
3. Combine all the other ingredients in a mixing bowl
4. Dip the slices of bread into the mixing bowl, covering all sides
5. Place the bread onto the parchment paper, inside the air fryer
6. Cook for 5 minutes on each side

Burgers For Breakfast

Servings - 2
Calories - 402, protein - 4g, fat - 3g, carbs - 21g

Ingredients
- 8 skinless sausages
- Salt and pepper for seasoning

Method
1. Preheat your air fryer to 260C/500F
2. Take a bowl and mash up the sausages
3. Add a little salt and pepper and combine again
4. Use your hands to create patties out of the sausage mixture
5. Place the patties into the air fryer cook for 8 minutes

Cheesy "Oven" Eggs

Servings - 2
Calories - 303, protein - 4g, fat - 2.6g, carbs - 21g

Ingredients
- 140g/5oz smoked gouda cheese
- 4 medium eggs
- Salt and pepper for seasoning
- 2 ramekin dishes, sprayed with a little cooking oil

Method
1. Preheat the air fryer to 350C/650F
2. Cut the cheese into small pieces
3. Crack an egg into each of the ramekin dishes and top with half the cheese in each one
4. Season to your liking and arrange inside the air fryer
5. Cook for 15 minutes, making sure the eggs are to your liking before serving

Vegetable Hash Browns

Servings - 4
Calories - 206, protein - 5g, fat - 2g, carbs - 40g

Ingredients

- 2 tbsp olive oil
- 4 potatoes, grated
- 2 tbsp bicarbonate of soda
- 1 tsp cayenne pepper
- 1 onion, chopped
- 1 red pepper, chopped
- 1 green pepper, chopped
- 1 tbsp salt
- 1 tbsp black pepper

Method

1. Take a large mixing bowl and fill with water. Add the potatoes
2. Add the bicarbonate of soda and set aside for 30 minutes
3. Preheat the air fryer to 200ºC/390F
4. Drain the bowl and remove the potatoes, patting dry, Place them in another bowl
5. Add the oil and the spices to the bowl and combine well
6. Transfer the potatoes to the air fryer basket
7. Cook for 10 minutes
8. Give the potatoes a shake before adding the onions and peppers
9. Cook for a further 10 minutes

Bacon & Mozzarella Toast

Servings - 2
Calories - 446, protein - 21g, fat - 21g, carbs - 23g

Ingredients

- 4 slices of sandwich bread
- 1 tbsp butter, melted
- 5 slices of bacon, cooked
- 2 slices of cheddar cheese
- 2 slices of mozzarella cheese

Method

1. Spread the butter onto one side of each slice of bread
2. Set the air fryer to 170°C/330F
3. Place the bread into the fryer, with the buttered side down
4. Place the cheddar on top, the bacon, mozzarella, and top with the other slice of bread. The buttered side should face upwards
5. Cook for 4 minutes
6. Turn over and cook for another 3 minutes

Egg & Ham Cups

Servings - 4
Calories - 82, protein - 4g, fat - 5g, carbs -11g

Ingredients
- 8 slices of sandwich bread, toasted
- Butter for greasing
- 2 slices of ham
- 4 eggs
- Salt and pepper for seasoning
- 4 ramekin dishes, greased

Method
1. Preheat the air fryer to 160°C/320F
2. Take a rolling pin and flatten the toast
3. Place two slices of toast into each ramekin
4. Line the inside of each dish with ham
5. Crack one egg into each dish and season
6. Place the ramekins into the air fryer basket and for 15 minutes
7. Cool before serving

Scrambled Eggs With Cheese

Servings - 1
Calories - 109, protein - 9g, fat - 8g, carbs - 3.5g

Ingredients

- 1 tbsp butter
- 2 tbsp milk
- 2 eggs
- 100g/3.5oz cheese, grated
- Salt and pepper for seasoning

Method

1. Preheat the air fryer to 220C/420F
2. Add the butter and cook until melted
3. Take a bowl and combine the eggs and milk with a little seasoning
4. Pour the mixture into the fryer and cook for 3 minutes, scrambling gently
5. Add the cheese and continue to cook for another 2 minutes

Cheesy Chorizo Frittata

Servings - 2
Calories - 401, protein - 21g, fat - 24g, carbs - 16g

Ingredients

- 1 tbsp olive oil
- 3 eggs
- 1 chorizo sausage, sliced
- 1 boiled potato, cut into cubes
- 50g/1.7oz feta cheese
- 50g/1.7oz sweetcorn
- A pinch of salt

Method

1. Preheat the air fryer to 180°C/350F
2. Add a little olive oil to the basket and allow to warm up
3. Add the potato, sweetcorn and chorizo
4. Cook until the sausage has browned
5. In a separate bowl, combine the eggs with a little seasoning
6. Pour the mixture into the pan with the crumbled feta on top
7. Cook for 5 minutes
8. Slice before serving

Swiss Cheese Breakfast Sandwich

Servings - 4
Calories - 244, protein - 2g, fat - 5g, carbs - 28g

Ingredients

- 1 egg
- 1 tsp butter, melted
- 2 slices of sandwich bread
- 4 slices of Swiss cheese
- 4 slices of ham
- 4 slices of turkey
- 1/4 tsp vanilla extract
- A pinch of powdered sugar

Method

1. Preheat the air fryer to 220C/420F
2. Combine the egg and vanilla extract in a bowl
3. Take a slice of bread and top with a slice of cheese, then ham, turkey and cheese again, topping with another slice of bread
4. Press the sandwich down
5. Brush a piece of foil with butter
6. Dip your sandwich into the egg mixture and make sure that it's coated on both sides
7. Place it on the foil to rest for a minute
8. Place in the air fryer and cook for 3 minutes
9. Turn over and cook for 3 minutes on the other side
10. Slice before serving

Joseph Biggs

Spicy Breakfast Wrap

Servings - 2
Calories - 503, protein - 2.3g, fat - 4g, carbs - 28g

Ingredients

- 25g/0.8oz cooked pinto beans
- 2 tortillas
- 2 corn tortillas, crushed
- 1 jalapeño pepper, sliced
- 4 tbsp ranchero sauce
- 1 avocado, sliced

Method

1. Preheat your air fryer to 190°C/370F
2. Take your tortillas and add the jalapeño, ranchero sauce, crushed corn tortillas, avocado, and pinto beans
3. Fold the wrap to make sure all the ingredients stay inside
4. Carefully add each wrap into your fryer and cook for 6 minutes
5. Once cooked, carefully take the wraps out of the air fryer and transfer to the oven
6. Cook at 180°C/350F for another 5 minutes
7. Then, transfer to a frying pan and cook on a low heat to add more crisp. This shouldn't take more than 2 minutes Turn over and do the same to the other side

Fruity Breakfast Muffins

Servings - 12
Calories - 310, protein - 6g, fat - 7g, carbs - 52g

Ingredients

- 2 tbsp of cooking oil
- 2 eggs
- 315g/11oz self-raising flour
- 65g/2oz sugar
- 120ml/0.5 cups of double/heavy cream
- 125g/4.4oz blueberries
- The zest and juice of a lemon
- 1 tsp vanilla

Method

1. Preheat your air fryer to 150°C/300F
2. Combine the self-raising flour and sugar in a small bowl
3. In a separate bowl, combine the oil, juice, eggs, vanilla, and cream
4. Add the wet mixture to the flour mixture and combine
5. Fold in the blueberries carefully with a plastic spatula
6. Use silicone muffin holders if you have them. Carefully spoon the mixture into the muffin holders
7. Place the muffin holders into the air fryer basket and cook for 10 minutes
8. Check the muffins the halfway point. If they're cooking too fast, turn the heat down
9. Allow to cool before removing from the muffin holders

Joseph Biggs

Stuffed Bell Peppers

Servings - 2
Calories - 154, protein - 10g, fat - 9g, carbs - 3g

Ingredients
- 1 tsp olive oil
- 1 large bell pepper, deseeded and halved
- 4 eggs
- Salt and pepper for seasoning

Method
1. Preheat your air fryer to 200ºC/390F
2. Rub some of the olive oil onto the edges of the olives
3. Add one egg into each pepper and a little seasoning
4. Create a trivet inside your air fryer basket, so the peppers don't fall over
5. Carefully place the peppers inside
6. Cook for 13 minutes, checking regularly
7. Season once more before serving

Homemade Breakfast Bagels

Servings - 2
Calories - 233, protein - 2g, fat - 4g, carbs - 28g

Ingredients

- 1 egg, beaten
- 170g/6oz self-raising flour
- 120ml/0.5 cups of plain yogurt

Method

1. Preheat your air fryer to 170ºC/330F
2. Combine the flour and the yogurt in a large bowl and create a dough
3. Cover a flat surface some flour and turn the dough out onto the floured surface
4. Divide the dough into four balls, even in size
5. Roll each ball out into a rope shape
6. Form a bagel from the rope shape
7. Brush the beaten egg over each bagel, covering completely to avoid burning
8. Arrange the bagels inside your fryer, keeping them on one layer and avoiding overlaps
9. Cook for 10 minutes
10. Allow to cool completely before serving

Sweet Potato Hash

Servings - 6
Calories - 190, protein - 3g, fat - 5g, carbs - 31g

Ingredients
- 2 tbsp olive oil
- 2 sweet potatoes, cubed
- 1 tbsp smoked paprika
- 2 slices of bacon, chopped
- Salt and pepper for seasoning

Method
1. Preheat your air fryer to 200ºC/390F
2. Take a large mixing bowl and add the olive oil
3. Add the potatoes, bacon, and seasoning. Toss and make sure everything is coated
4. Transfer into the air fryer and cook for 12-16 minutes
5. After 10 minutes, give everything a stir and keep stirring every so often for the next 5 minutes

Berry Pockets

Servings - 1
Calories - 255, protein - 3g, fat - 5g, carbs - 30g

Ingredients
- 1 egg
- 1 tbsp soft cream cheese
- 2 slices of sandwich bread
- 1 tbsp raspberry jam
- 1 tbsp milk

Method
1. Spray the inside of the fryer with a little oil and preheat the air fryer to 190°C/370F
2. Take one slice of the bread and add a tablespoon of jam into the middle
3. Take another slice of bread and add the cream cheese in the centre again
4. Spread the jam and the cream cheese over the bread but avoid the edges
5. Place one slice of bread over the other to make a sandwich
6. Whisk the eggs and the milk together in a small mixing bowl
7. Dip the sandwich into the egg and carefully place inside your air fryer
8. Cook for 5 minutes before turning and cooking for a further 2 minutes on the other side

Air Fryer Lunch Recipes

At lunch time you might be in a rush. Busy work days, looking after the kids, appointments to get to, the list goes on. So, you want to make a delicious lunch that is low on health impact and high on flavour. It's time to grab your air fryer and create these mouthwatering lunch recipes!

Peppery Chicken Wings

Servings - 2
Calories - 346, protein - 7g, fat - 5g, carbs - 30g

Ingredients

- 1kg/2.2lb chicken wings
- 3 tbsp butter, melted
- 1 tsp honey
- 1/4 tsp cayenne pepper
- 2 tsp lemon pepper seasoning, plus an extra 1tsp for the space

Method

1. Preheat the air fryer to 260C/550F
2. Combine the lemon pepper seasoning and cayenne pepper in a bowl
3. Cover the chicken in the seasoning, ensuring everything is evenly coated
4. Arrange the chicken in the air fryer
5. Cook for 20 minutes, turning over at the halfway point
6. Turn the temperature up to 300C/570F and cook for another 6 minutes
7. Combine the melted butter with the honey and the rest of the seasoning mixture
8. Once the chicken wings have cooked, removed them from the air fryer basket
9. Pour the sauce over the top of the wings while they're still hot

Mediterranean Chicken Balls

Servings - 4
Calories - 336, protein - 18g, fat - 6g, carbs - 31g

Ingredients

- 500g/17oz ground chicken
- 1 large egg
- 1.5 tbsp garlic paste
- 1 tbsp dried oregano
- 1 tsp dried onion powder
- 1 tsp lemon zest
- Salt and pepper for seasoning

Method

1. Preheat your air fryer to 260C/500F
2. Combine all ingredients into a large bowl, making sure everything is totally mixed together
3. Create meatballs using your hands. With this mixture, you should be able to create 12 evenly sized balls
4. Place the meatballs inside the air fryer, making sure there is some space between them
5. Cook for 9 minutes

Breaded Chicken Tenders

Servings - 4
Calories - 213, protein - 26g, fat - 11g, carbs - 9g

Ingredients

- 2 tbsp olive oil
- 8 frozen chicken tenders
- 1 egg, beaten
- 150g/5oz dried breadcrumbs

Method

1. Preheat the air fryer to 175C/340F
2. Take a large bowl and combine the breadcrumbs and oil
3. Take one tender and it into the beaten egg, and then dip into the breadcrumb mixture, making sure it is fully coated
4. Carefully arrange the tender in the fryer basket
5. Repeat with the rest of the tenders
6. When placing them inside the air fryer, make sure they don't touch, and keep them on one even layer
7. Cook for 12 minutes
8. Check the chicken is cooked through before serving

Popcorn Shrimp With a Kick

Servings - 2
Calories - 300, protein - 12g, fat - 18g, carbs - 11g

Ingredients

- 300g/10oz popcorn shrimps, frozen
- 1 tsp cayenne pepper
- Salt and pepper for seasoning

Method

1. Preheat the air fryer to 220C/420F
2. Place the shrimp inside the air fryer in an even layer
3. Cook for 6 minutes. At 3 minutes, shake the shrimp well and continue to cook until the full 6 minutes
4. Remove the shrimp when crispy
5. Before serving, season with the cayenne pepper, salt and pepper, to your liking

Panky Calamari

Servings - 2
Calories - 406, protein - 20g, fat - 20g, carbs - 21g

Ingredients

- 250g/8.5oz plain flour
- 200ml/0.8 cups of buttermilk
- 1 egg
- 500g/17oz squid rings
- 500g/17oz panko breadcrumbs
- 2 tbsp pepper
- 2 tbsp salt

Method

1. Preheat the air fryer at 150C/300F
2. Combine the buttermilk and egg in a large bowl and make sure everything is fully combined
3. Combine the salt, pepper, flour, and panko breadcrumbs in another bowl, making sure everything is mixed together
4. Dip the squid into the buttermilk, followed by the breadcrumbs. Make sure the squid is fully coated on all sides
5. Place in the air fryer basket, making sure they're arranged in an even layer and aren't touching
6. Cook for 12 minutes, until golden brown

Joseph Biggs

Lime Salmon Patties

Servings - 7
Calories - 503, fat - 22g, protein - 14g, carbs - 24g

Ingredients

- Cooking spray
- 2 eggs
- 1 large can of salmon, drained
- 30g/1oz panko breadcrumbs
- ¼ tsp salt
- 1 ½ tbsp brown sugar
- 1 ½ tbsp Thai red curry paste
- Zest of 1 lime

Method

1. Preheat your air fryer to 180C/356F
2. Combine all ingredients together in a large bowl, until you get a smooth mixture
3. Create patties by using your hands. You should aim for 1" thick, evenly sized patties
4. Spray the patties with a little cooking spray and arrange inside the air fryer, in an even layer
5. Cook for 4 minutes on one side, before turning and cooking for another 4 minutes on the other side

Steak Bites

Servings - 4
Calories - 316, protein - 31g, fat - 51g, carbs - 27g

Ingredients
- 500g/17oz steak, cut into cubes
- 500g/17oz potato chips
- 2 eggs, beaten
- 100g/3.5oz flour
- Salt and pepper for seasoning

Method
1. Preheat your air fryer to 260C/500F
2. Arrange the chips into your food processor and process unit you get fine crumbs
3. Combine the flour with salt and pepper in a large bowl
4. In another bowl, add the chips crumbs
5. Add the beaten egg to another bowl
6. Take the steak cubes and dip first in the flour, the egg, and the chip crumbs, making sure everything is fully coated on all sides
7. Arrange the steak bites into the air fryer and cook for 9 minutes

Joseph Biggs

Beef & Courgette (Zucchini) Frittata

Servings - 2
Calories - 214, protein - 13g, fat - 31g, carbs - 20g

Ingredients

- 250g/8.8oz ground beef
- 250g/8.8oz grated cheese
- 4 hash browns, shredded
- 8 eggs
- Half an onion, diced
- 1 courgette/zucchini, diced
- Salt and pepper for seasoning

Method

1. Preheat the air fryer to 260C/500F
2. Crumble the ground beef and place it in the air fryer basket
3. Add the onion and combine well
4. Cook for 3 minutes
5. Stir the mixture and cook for another 2 minutes
6. Remove the mixture and give the tray a clean
7. Add the courgette/zucchini to the air fryer
8. Cook for 3 minutes, stirring occasionally to make sure it doesn't stick
9. Add to the meat mixture and combine well
10. Combine the cheese, hash browns, and eggs in a large mixing bowl
11. Add the meat and courgette/zucchini to the bowl and season with a little salt and pepper
12. Transfer the mixture to a baking tray that will fit into your air fryer
13. Cook for 8 minutes
14. Cut lines in the top and continue to cook for a further 8 minutes
15. Allow to cool before cutting into slices

Lamb & Harissa Burgers

Servings - 4
Calories - 438, protein - 21g, fat - 31g, carbs - 4g

Ingredients

- 600g/21oz minced lamb
- 2 tbsp Moroccan spice
- 2 tsp garlic puree
- 1 tsp harissa paste
- Salt and pepper for seasoning

Method

1. Preheat the air fryer to 180C/350F
2. Take a large bowl and place all ingredients inside
3. Combine well to achieve a smooth mixture
4. Use your hands to create evenly sized patties
5. Place in the air fryer, making sure the patties don't touch and are on one even layer
6. Cook for 8 minutes

Swiss Cheese & Ham Sliders

Servings - 4
Calories - 411, protein - 31g, fat - 39g, carbs - 22g

Ingredients

- 8 slider bread rolls, halved
- 16 slices of Swiss cheese
- 16 slices of ham
- 5 tbsp mayonnaise
- 1 tsp onion powder
- 1/2 tsp paprika
- 1 tsp dill

Method

1. Preheat your air fryer to 220C/420F
2. Take your halved slider rolls and place 2 slices of ham on each
3. Top with 2 slices of the Swiss cheese
4. Combine the mayonnaise with the onion powder, dill, and paprika in a large mixing bowl
5. Add half a tablespoon of the sauce on top of each piece of cheese
6. Place the top on the bread slider to create a sandwich
7. Carefully place the sandwich inside the air fryer basket
8. Cook for 5 minutes before turning over and cooking for another 5 minutes

Joseph Biggs

Potato & Carrot Burgers

Servings - 12
Calories - 206, protein - 21g, fat - 20g, carbs - 23g

Ingredients
- 1 tbsp oil
- 100ml hot water
- 150g/5oz instant mashed potato
- 50g/1.7oz frozen peas and carrots, defrosted
- 2 tbsp coriander
- ½ tsp turmeric
- ½ tsp cumin seeds
- ¼ tsp ground cumin
- ½ tsp cayenne
- ½ tsp salt

Method
1. Spray the inside of the air fryer with a little cooking spread and preheat to 200C/390F
2. Take a large bowl and add all the ingredients inside
3. Combine everything together well and place to one side to rest for 10 minutes
4. Use your hands to create 12 evenly sized patties
5. Arrange the patties inside the air fryer, ensuring they don't touch and they're all on an even layer
6. Cook for 10 minutes

Italian Ravioli

Servings - 4
Calories - 206, protein - 12g, fat - 14g, carbs - 30g

Ingredients

- 1 tbsp olive oil
- Half a pack of ravioli, frozen works best
- 200ml/0.8 cups of buttermilk
- 200g/7oz Italian breadcrumbs
- 5 tbsp marinara sauce

Method

1. Preheat the air fryer to 220C/428F
2. Take a large bowl and add the buttermilk
3. Take another bowl and add the breadcrumbs
4. Take each piece of ravioli and dip it into the buttermilk then into the breadcrumbs, making sure everything is coated evenly on all sides
5. Add the ravioli to the air fryer and arrange in an even layer
6. Cook for 7 minutes
7. At the halfway point, add a small amount of oil, stir slightly and continue cooking to finish
8. Serve with the marinara sauce

Onion Dumplings

Servings - 2
Calories - 309, protein - 2g, fat - 8g, carbs - 11g

Ingredients

- 1 tbsp olive oil
- 14 pierogi dumplings, frozen
- 1 onion, sliced
- 1 tsp sugar

Method

1. Fill a large saucepan with water and bring to the boil
2. Cook the dumplings for 5 minutes
3. Once cooked, removed and drain carefully
4. Add a small amount of oil to the air fryer basket and preheat to 220C/428F
5. Cook the onion for 12 minutes, giving it a stir every so often
6. After 5 minutes, add the sugar to the air fryer and combine well
7. Remove the onions from the air fryer and set aside
8. Add the cooked dumplings to the air fryer and cook for 4 minutes
9. Increase the temperature up to 270C/518F and cook for 3 minutes extra
10. Combine the dumplings with the onions and serve

Italian Aubergine (Eggplant) Parmesan

Servings - 2
Calories - 246, protein - 21g, fat - 25g, carbs - 23g

Ingredients

- 1 egg
- 1 tbsp water
- 1 large aubergine/eggplant, sliced
- 4 slices of wholewheat bread - create breadcrumbs out of these
- 3 tbsp Parmesan cheese, grated
- 30g/1oz mozzarella cheese, grated
- 1 tsp Italian seasoning
- 3 tbsp whole wheat flour
- 5 tbsp marinara sauce
- Salt for seasoning

Method

1. Take the aubergine/eggplant and season both sides. Set to one side for 30 minutes
2. Preheat the air fryer to 270C/518F
3. Combine the egg, flour, and water in a bowl and make sure everything is mixed together well
4. Take a plate and add the breadcrumbs, parmesan, and Italian seasoning, combining well to create a coating
5. Dip the aubergine/eggplant into the egg mixture and then the breadcrumbs, making sure it is fully coated on all sides
6. Carefully arrange the aubergine/eggplant into the air fryer basket and cook for 8 minutes
7. Add the marinara sauce and mozzarella on top and cook for another 2 minutes

Spicy Buffalo Wings

Servings - 4
Calories - 228, fat - 41g, protein - 20g, carbs - 7g

Ingredients

- 500g/17oz chicken wings
- 2 tbsp vinegar
- 1 tbsp olive oil
- 75g/2.6oz butter
- 5 tbsp cayenne pepper sauce
- ¼ tsp cayenne pepper
- 1 tsp garlic powder

Method

1. Preheat your air fryer to 182C/350F
2. Place the chicken wings into a large bowl
3. Drizzle oil over the wings, tossing to coat evenly
4. Place the wings inside the air fryer basket and cook for 25 minutes
5. Turn the wings and cook for another 5 minutes
6. Take a saucepan and heat over a medium temperature on your hob
7. Add the hot pepper sauce, butter, vinegar, garlic powder, and cayenne pepper, mixing together well
8. Pour the sauce over the wings and flip to coat, before serving

Air Fryer Dinner Recipes

After a busy day at work, the last thing you want to do is start grabbing multiple pans and cooking full meals. Your air fryer has you covered. You can easily make a truly sumptuous meal with your appliance, with less stress and a lot of flavour. When you add meal planning into the equation, everything becomes even easier!

Which of these fantastic air fryer dinner recipes will you try first?

Mushroom & Turkey Cutlets

Servings - 2
Calories - 406, protein - 26g, fat - 20g, carbs - 17g

Ingredients

- 160ml/0.6 cups of milk
- 2 turkey cutlets
- 1 tbsp butter, melted
- 1 can of cream of mushroom sauce
- Salt and pepper for seasoning

Method

1. Preheat the air fryer to 220C/428F
2. Brush the turkey cults with the butter and add a little seasoning
3. Place in the air fryer, leaving a little space between them and cook for 11 minutes
4. Take a saucepan and add the mushroom soup and milk
5. Cook over a medium heat for around 10 minutes, stirring occasionally
6. Pour the sauce over the turkey cutlets before serving

Joseph Biggs

Spicy Chicken Chimichangas

Servings - 6
Calories - 406, protein - 21g, fat - 22g, carbs - 26g

Ingredients

- 100g/3.5oz shredded cooked chicken
- 6 flour tortillas
- 150g/5oz nacho cheese
- 1 jalapeño pepper, chopped
- 60g/2oz refried beans
- 5 tbsp salsa
- 0.5 tsp chill powder
- 1 tsp cumin
- Salt and pepper for seasoning

Method

1. Spray the air fryer with a little cooking spray and preheat to 200C/390F
2. Add all of the ingredients into a large bowl and combine well
3. Take your tortillas and add ⅓ of the filling to each
4. Roll the tortillas into a burrito shape
5. Place the tortillas in the air fryer in one even layer
6. Cook for 7 minutes

Furikake & Mayo Salmon

Servings - 2
Calories - 309, protein - 13g, fat - 21g, carbs - 22g

Ingredients

- 1 salmon fillet
- 150ml/0.6 cups of mayonnaise
- 2 tbsp furikake
- 1 tbsp soy sauce
- Salt and pepper for seasoning

Method

1. Preheat your air fryer to 230C/446F
2. Combine the mayonnaise and soy sauce in a small bowl
3. Season the salmon on both sides
4. Place the salmon into the air fryer with the skin side down
5. Brush the mayonnaise mixture on top of the salmon evenly
6. Sprinkle the furikake on top of the salmon
7. Cook for 10 minutes

Breaded Fish Fillets With Ranch

Servings - 4
Calories - 311, protein - 36g, fat - 12g, carbs - 7g

Ingredients
- 4 fish fillets - your choice
- 2 tbsp oil
- 200g/7oz breadcrumbs
- 30g/1oz ranch-style dressing mix
- 2 eggs, beaten
- Lemon wedges to garnish

Method
1. Preheat your air fryer to 180C/356F
2. Take a bowl and combine the breadcrumbs and ranch dressing
3. Add the oil until the mix becomes smooth
4. Dip the fish into the breadcrumb mixture, making sure it is covered evenly on all sides
5. Carefully place the fish into the air fryer and cook for 13 minutes

Traditional Beef Wellington

Servings - 4
Calories - 202, protein - 31g, fat - 21g, carbs - 28g

Ingredients
- 600g/21oz beef fillet
- 300g/10oz chicken liver pate
- 1 egg, beaten
- 500g/17oz shortcrust pastry
- Salt and pepper for seasoning

Method
1. Season the beef with a little salt and pepper
2. Wrap the beef in cling film and place in the refrigerator for 1 hour
3. Meanwhile, take the shortcrust pastry and roll it out
4. Brush the edges of the pastry with beaten egg
5. Spread the pate over the pastry in an even layer
6. Take the beef out of the refrigerator and remove the clingfilm
7. Place the beef in the centre of the pastry and wrap it around, sealing around the meat
8. Preheat your air fryer to 160C/320F
9. Place the beef into the air fryer and cook for 35 minutes

Joseph Biggs

Coconut & Ginger Beef

Servings - 2
Calories - 336, protein - 12g, fat - 31g, carbs - 13g

Ingredients

- 600g/21oz steak, sliced thinly
- 25ml/0.2 cups of water
- 100g/3.5oz brown sugar
- ½ tbsp minced garlic
- 1 tbsp coconut oil
- 2 red peppers, sliced
- 25g/0.8oz liquid aminos
- ¼ tsp pepper
- ½ tsp ground ginger
- 1 tsp red pepper flakes
- ¼ tsp salt

Method

1. Take a saucepan and add the coconut oil, melting over a medium heat
2. Add the sliced red pepper and cook until soft
3. Take another pan to add the aminos, brown sugar, ginger, garlic, and pepper flakes, combining well
4. Bring the pan to the boil, then turn the temperature down and simmer for 10 mins
5. Preheat the air fryer to 200C/392F
6. Season the steak with salt and pepper
7. Place the steak inside the air fryer and cook for 10 minutes.
8. Turn the steak and cook for a further 5 minutes until crispy
9. Transfer the steak to the pepper mixture and combing with the ginger sauce

Classic Beef Satay

Servings - 2
Calories - 446, protein - 21g, fat - 16g, carbs - 15g

Ingredients

- 2 tbsp oil
- 400g/14oz steak, cut into strips
- 25g/0.8oz roasted peanuts
- 1 tbsp fish sauce
- 1 tsp sriracha sauce
- 1 tbsp soy sauce
- 1 tbsp sugar
- 200g/7oz fresh coriander, sliced
- 1 tsp ground coriander/cilantro
- 1 tbsp minced ginger
- 1 tbsp minced garlic

Method

1. Take a large bowl and add the oil, fish sauce, soy, ginger, garlic, sugar sriracha, coriander, and ¼ cup coriander/cilantro. Combine well
2. Add the steak to the bowl, combine and marinate for 30 minutes
3. Preheat the air fryer to 200C/392F
4. Add the steak to the air fryer and cook for 8 minutes
5. Transfer the steak onto a plate and top with the remaining coriander/cilantro and chopped peanuts

Mustard & Garlic Pork Tenderloin

Servings - 2
Calories - 497, protein - 30g, fat - 37g, carbs - 22g

Ingredients

- 3 tbsp olive oil
- 1 pork tenderloin
- 1 tbsp dijon mustard
- 3 tbsp soy sauce
- 2 minced garlic cloves
- 2 tbsp brown sugar
- Salt and pepper for seasoning

Method

1. Take a large bowl and combine all the ingredients, except for the pork
2. Pour the mixture into a ziplock bag and then add the pork, sealing the bag
3. Place the bag into the refrigerator for 30minutes
4. Preheat your air fryer to 260C/500F
5. Remove the pork from the bag and place it in the air fryer
6. Cook for 25 minutes, being sure to turn the pork over at the halfway point
7. Remove and rest for 5 minutes
8. Slice into pieces

Balsamic Pork Chops with Raspberry

Servings - 4
Calories - 569, protein - 31g, fat - 30g, carbs - 32g

Ingredients

- 2 eggs
- 4 pork chops
- 30ml/0.2 cups of milk
- 30ml/0.2 cups of balsamic vinegar
- 1 tbsp orange juice
- 250g/8.8oz panko breadcrumbs
- 250g/8.8oz pecans, finely chopped
- 2 tbsp brown sugar
- 2 tbsp raspberry jam

Method

1. Preheat the air fryer to 200C/390F
2. Take a medium mixing bowl and combine the eggs and milk
3. Take a separate bowl and combine the breadcrumbs and pecans
4. Take the pork chops and coat in the flour, egg and then the breadcrumbs
5. Place in the air fryer and cook for 12 minutes until golden, being sure to turn at the halfway point
6. Take a pan and place the remaining ingredients inside
7. Simmer over a medium heat for around 6 minutes
8. Serve the sauce with the pork chops

Balsamic Gnocchi Caprese

Servings - 2
Calories - 206, protein - 20g, fat - 15g, carbs - 20g

Ingredients

- 2 tbsp olive oil
- 1 pack of gnocchi
- 150g/5oz cherry tomatoes, halved
- 150g/5oz Parmesan, grated
- 200g/7oz mini mozzarella balls
- 2 tbsp balsamic vinegar
- 3 cloves of garlic, pressed
- 200g/7oz basil, chopped
- Salt and pepper for seasoning

Method

1. Preheat the air fryer to 220C/428F
2. Take a large bowl and add the gnocchi, cherry tomatoes, balsamic vinegar, oil, garlic, and seasoning. Combine everything well
3. Transfer the mixture to the air fryer basket
4. Cook for 10 minutes, shaking the basket every few minutes
5. Once cooked, transfer everything to a large mixing bowl
6. Add the Parmesan cheese and combine to coat
7. Add the mozzarella and basil, combining well before serving

Garlic & Citrus Cauliflower

Servings - 2
Calories - 376, protein - 20g, fat - 15g, carbs - 12g

Ingredients

- 2 tsp olive oil
- Head of cauliflower, cut into florets
- 200ml/0.8 cups of water
- 200g/7oz flour
- 2 garlic cloves, minced
- 1 tsp minced ginger
- 150ml/0.6 cups of orange juice
- 3 tbsp white vinegar
- 1/2 tsp red pepper flakes
- 1 tsp sesame oil
- 100g/3.5oz brown sugar
- 3 tbsp soy sauce
- 1 tbsp cornstarch
- 2 tbsp water
- 1 tsp salt

Method

1. Preheat the air fryer to 220C/428F
2. Add the water, salt, and flour into a large mixing bowl and combine
3. Dip each floret of cauliflower into the mixture and place it in the air fryer basket afterwards
4. Cook for 15 minutes
5. Meanwhile, make the orange sauce. Add all the remaining ingredients into a pan and combine
6. Heat over a medium temperature and allow to simmer for 3 minutes. The sauce should thicken
7. Drizzle the sauce over the cauliflower before serving

Falafel Patties

Servings - 2
Calories - 700, protein - 32g, fat - 27g, carbs - 90g

Ingredients

- 1 can of chickpeas
- 4 tbsp soft cheese
- 1 onion
- The rind and juice of 1 lemon
- 140g/5oz oats
- 3 tbsp Greek yogurt
- 28g/0.9oz cheddar cheese, grated
- 28g/0.9oz feta cheese
- 1 tbsp garlic puree
- 1 tbsp coriander
- 1 tbsp oregano
- 1 tbsp parsley
- Salt and pepper to taste

Method

1. Place the chickpeas, lemon rind, garlic, onion, and seasonings into a food processor and blitz until coarse
2. Preheat the air fryer to 180C/350F
3. Transfer the mix to a bowl and stir in half the soft cheese, feta, and cheddar cheese
4. Use your hands to form patties
5. Place the oats onto a plate and roll the patties on the plate to coat well
6. Place in the air fryer and cook for 8 minutes
7. Take a bowl and combine the remaining soft cheese, greek yogurt, and lemon juice to make the serving sauce

Tikka Paneer

Servings - 2
Calories - 306, protein - 13g, fat - 20g, carbs - 21g

Ingredients

- 1 tbsp olive oil
- 200ml/0.8 cups of yogurt
- 1 chopped onion
- 1 chopped green pepper
- 1 chopped red pepper
- 1 chopped yellow pepper
- 250g paneer cheese, cubed
- 1 tsp ginger garlic paste
- 1 tsp red chilli powder
- 1 tsp garam masala
- 1 tsp turmeric powder
- 1 tbsp dried fenugreek leaves
- The juice of 1 lemon
- 2 tbsp chopped coriander/cilantro
- 8 metal skewers

Method

1. Combine the yogurt, garlic paste, red chilli powder, turmeric powder, garam masala, lemon juice, fenugreek, and chopped coriander/cilantro in a bowl. Place to one side to rest for 10 minutes
2. Add the cheese and coat well
3. Leave to marinate for 2 hours in the refrigerator
4. Preheat your air fryer to 220C/428F
5. Take 8 metal skewers and thread the peppers, onions, and cheese alternately
6. Drizzle a little oil over the top of the skewers
7. Arrange in the air fryer and cook for 3 minutes
8. Turn over and cook for a further 3 minutes

Creamy Mushroom Pasta

Servings - 4
Calories - 400, protein - 11g, fat - 31g, carbs - 9g

Ingredients

- 250g/8.8oz mushrooms, sliced
- 300g/10oz cooked pasta - your choice
- 1 onion, chopped
- 75g/2.6oz double cream/heavy cream
- 30g/1oz parmesan, grated
- 70g/2.5oz mascarpone
- 2 tsp minced garlic
- ½ tsp red pepper flakes
- 1 tsp dried thyme
- 1 tsp ground black pepper
- 1 tsp salt

Method

1. Take a bowl and combine all ingredients
2. Preheat the air fryer to 175C/347F
3. Grease a 7x3 inch pan and add the mixture inside
4. Place the pan into the air fryer and cook for 15 minutes
5. Halfway through, give the mixture a stir
6. Pour the sauce over the cooked pasta, stir and sprinkle with the parmesan

Garlic Buttermilk Chicken

Servings - 4
Calories - 305, fat - 41g, protein - 20g, carbs - 7g

Ingredients

- 500g/17oz chicken thighs, boneless
- 75g/2.6oz all-purpose flour
- ½ tsp brown sugar
- 180ml/0.7 cups of buttermilk
- 40g/1.4oz tapioca flour
- 1 egg, beaten
- ½ tsp garlic salt
- 1 tsp garlic powder
- ½ tsp paprika
- ½ tsp onion powder
- ¼ tsp oregano
- Salt and pepper for seasoning

Method

1. Combine the buttermilk and hot sauce in a mixing bowl
2. Add the garlic salt, tapioca flour, and black pepper into a plastic bag and shake to combine
3. Take the chicken thighs and add to the buttermilk to coat
4. Coat in the tapioca mixture, the egg, and then the flour
5. Preheat the air fryer to 190C/374F
6. Cook the chicken thighs for 10 minutes
7. Make sure the chicken is white in the middle before serving

EXCLUSIVE BONUS

40 Weight Loss Recipes

&

14 Days Meal Plan

Scan the QR-Code and receive the FREE download:

Air Fryer Dessert Recipes

It's entirely possible to enjoy a dessert without having to start beating eggs together and using your blender. Your air fryer can cook fantastic dessert recipes too.

So, what do you fancy for dessert today? Maybe one of these recipe choices will tickle your tastebuds?

Key Lime Cupcakes

Servings - 6
Calories - 208, protein - 7g, fat - 11g, carbs - 14g

Ingredients

- 2 eggs, plus 1 egg yolk
- 200g/7oz soft cheese
- 250g/8oz Greek yogurt
- Juice and rind of 2 limes
- 60ml/0.25 cups of caster sugar
- 1 tsp vanilla essence
- 6 cupcake cases

Method

1. Take a bowl and combine the yogurt and soft cheese until smooth
2. Add the eggs and combine
3. Add the lime juice and rind, vanilla, and caster sugar and combine again
4. Fill the cupcake cases with the mixture and allow to rest
5. Preheat the air fryer to 160C/320F
6. Place the cupcakes into the air fryer and cook for 10 minutes
7. Increase the heat to 180C/356F for another 10 minutes
8. Place the remaining mixture into a piping bag
9. Once the cupcakes have cooled, pipe the mixture on top of the cupcakes and place in the refrigerator to set

Chocolate & Vanilla Biscuits

Servings - 6
Calories - 304, protein - 4g, fat -16g, carbs - 50g

Ingredients

- 50g/1.7oz milk chocolate
- 1 egg, beaten
- 225g/7.9oz self-raising flour
- 100g/3.5oz sugar
- 100g/3.5oz butter
- 1 tsp vanilla essence

Method

1. Preheat the air fryer to 180C/356F
2. Take a bowl and rub together the flour, butter, and sugar
3. Add the egg and vanilla, and combine to form a dough
4. Divide the dough into 6 even pieces and use your hands to form balls
5. Place in the air fryer cook for 15 minutes
6. Melt the chocolate over a pan of hot water
7. Once melted, dip the cooked biscuits into the chocolate, and allow to set

Coconut Fried Bananas

Servings - 8
Calories - 150, protein - 20g, fat - 21g, carbs - 17g

Ingredients

- 4 bananas, halved - make sure they're ripe
- 2 tbsp flour
- 2 tbsp rice flour
- 2 tbsp cornflour
- 2 tbsp desiccated coconut
- ½ tsp baking powder
- ½ tsp cardamon powder
- A pinch of salt

Method

1. Take a bowl and add all the dry ingredients. Combine well
2. Add a little water at a time and combine to form a batter
3. Preheat the air fryer to 200C/392F
4. Line the air fryer with parchment paper and spray with cooking spray
5. Dip each banana piece in the batter mix and place it in the air fryer
6. Cook for 10 minutes, turning at the halfway point

Joseph Biggs

Citrus & Chocolate Fondant

Servings - 4
Calories - 411, protein - 14g, fat - 37g, carbs - 31g

Ingredients
- The rind and juice of 1 orange
- 2 eggs
- 115g/4oz dark chocolate, melted
- 2 tbsp self-raising flour
- 4 tbsp caster sugar
- 115g/4oz butter
- 4 ramekin dishes, greased

Method
1. Preheat the air fryer to 180C/356F
2. Take a bowl and beat the eggs and sugar until the mixture is fluffy and pale
3. Add the orange juice and rind to the melted chocolate and combine
4. Add the egg mixture and combine
5. Slowly sift the flour into the mixture and combine gently
6. Divide the mixture between the ramekin dishes
7. Place the dishes into the air fryer and cook for 12 minutes
8. Allow to cool slightly before serving

Chocolate Citrus Muffins

Servings - 12
Calories - 600, protein - 27g, fat - 25g, carbs - 30g

Ingredients
- 50ml/0.2 cups of milk
- 2 eggs
- The orange and rind of 1 large orange
- 1 tbsp honey
- 100g/3.5oz self-raising flour
- 110g/3.8oz caster sugar
- 50g/1.7oz butter
- 20g/0.7oz cocoa powder
- 1 tsp cocoa nibs
- 1tsp vanilla essence
- 12 muffin cases

Method
1. Preheat the air fryer to 180C/356F
2. Take a bowl and combine the flour, butter, and sugar
3. Add the cocoa, vanilla honey, orange juice and rind, and mix well
4. Take another bowl and add the egg and milk together
5. Add the flour mixture and combine again
6. Add 2 tbsp of the cake batter to each muffin case
7. Place in the air fryer and cook for 12 minutes

Classic Profiteroles

Servings - 9
Calories - 400, protein - 6g, fat - 28g, carbs - 30g

Ingredients

- 6 eggs
- 100g/3.5oz butter
- 200g/7oz plain flour
- 100g/3.5oz milk chocolate
- 2 tbsp double/heavy cream, whipped
- 300ml/1.2 cups of water
- 2 tsp vanilla extract
- 50g/1.7oz butter
- 2 tsp icing sugar

Method

1. Preheat the air fryer to 170C/338F
2. Take a medium saucepan and add the butter and water
3. Bring to the boil over a medium heat and remove once boiling
4. Stir in the flour slowly
5. Return to the heat, stirring constantly until a dough is formed
6. Slowly add the eggs and stir until the mixture is smooth
7. Create profiterole shapes with your hands out of the mixture
8. Place the profiteroles in the air fryer and cook for 10 minutes
9. Meanwhile, make the filling. Add the whipped cream (keep 2 tbsp to one side), vanilla and icing sugar to a bowl and whisk together
10. Then, create the topping by combining the butter, remaining whipped cream and butter and heating gently over a low heat until everything is melted together
11. Once the profiteroles are cool, add the filling to a piping bag and fill generously
12. Add a little of the topping and allow to set

New York Cheesecake

Servings - 8
Calories - 800, protein - 10g, fat - 50g, carbs - 80g

Ingredients

- 3 eggs
- 50ml/0.2 cups of quark
- 750g/26oz soft cheese
- 225g/7.9oz plain flour
- 100g/3.5oz brown sugar
- 100g/3.5oz butter
- 50g/1.7oz butter, melted
- 1 tbsp vanilla essence
- 250g/8oz sugar

Method

1. Preheat your air fryer to 180C/356F
2. Take a bowl and combine the flour, sugar, and 100g of the butter
3. Use your hands to create biscuit shapes
4. Place the biscuits into the air fryer and cook for 15 minutes
5. Grease a springform tin
6. Break the biscuits up and mix with the melted butter, combining well
7. Press down into the bottom of the springform tin to make the cheesecake base
8. Mix the soft cheese and sugar in a bowl until creamy, add the eggs and vanilla and mix
9. Slowly add the quark and combine
10. Pour the cheesecake batter into the pan and coat evenly
11. Place in your air fryer and cook for 30 minutes
12. Leave the cheesecake inside the air fryer for 30 minutes to cool
13. Transfer to the refrigerator for 6 hours

Creamy Cherry Pies

Servings - 6
Calories - 606, protein - 20g, fat - 21g, carbs - 27g

Ingredients

- 75g/2.6oz cherry pie filling
- 300g/10.5oz shortcrust pastry, rolled out
- ½ tsp milk
- 3 tbsp icing sugar
- Cooking spray

Method

1. Preheat the air fryer to 175C/347F and spray with a little cooking spray
2. Take the shortcrust pastry and use a cookie cutter to cut out 6 pie shapes
3. Add 1 ½ tbsp filling to the centre of each pie shape
4. Fold the dough over in half and seal around the edges with a fork
5. Place the pies into the air fryer and cook for 10 minutes
6. Mix icing sugar and milk together in a bowl and drizzle over the cooled pies before serving

Chocolate Soufflé

Servings - 2
Calories - 406, protein - 21g, fat - 27g, carbs - 23g

Ingredients

- 150g/5.2oz semi-sweet chocolate, chopped
- 60ml/0.25 cups of butter
- 2 eggs, separated
- 3 tbsp sugar
- ½ tsp vanilla extract
- 2 tbsp flour
- Icing sugar to serve
- 2 ramekin dishes, greased

Method

1. Add the butter and chocolate to a saucepan and melt over a low heat
2. In another bowl beat the egg yolks, add the sugar and vanilla, and combine well
3. Slowly add the chocolate, flour, and mix well
4. Preheat the air fryer to 165C/329F
5. Whisk the egg whites to soft peaks and gently fold into the chocolate mix a little at a time
6. Add the mix to ramekins and place in the air fryer
7. Cook for 14 minutes
8. Dust with icing sugar before serving

Joseph Biggs

Decadent Chocolate Cake

Servings - 2
Calories - 503, protein - 40g, fat - 79g, carbs - 25g

Ingredients

- 25g/0.8oz cocoa powder
- 3 eggs
- 75ml/0.3 cups of sour cream
- 225g/8oz flour
- 150g/5.2oz sugar
- 2 tsp vanilla extract
- ½ tsp baking soda
- 1 tsp baking powder

Method

1. Preheat the air fryer to 160C/320F
2. Mix all the ingredients together in a bowl
3. Pour into a greased baking tin and place inside the air fryer
4. Cook for 25 minutes

Strawberry "Pop-Tarts"

Servings - 12
Calories - 306, protein - 21g, fat - 27g, carbs - 20g

Ingredients

- 75ml/0.3 cups of ice-cold water
- 100g /3.5oz strawberry Jam
- 1 tsp coconut oil, melted
- 300g/10oz whole wheat flour
- 225g/7.9oz white flour
- ¼ tsp salt
- 2 tbsp light brown sugar
- 300g/10oz icing sugar
- 2 tbsp lemon juice
- Zest of 1 lemon
- 150g/5.2oz cold coconut oil
- 1 tsp vanilla extract
- ¼ tsp vanilla extract

Joseph Biggs

Method

1. Take a bowl and combine the two flours, salt, and sugar
2. Slowly mix in the cold coconut oil
3. Add 1 tsp vanilla and 1 tbsp of the ice-cold water at a time
4. Mix until a dough is formed
5. Preheat the air fryer to 200C/392F
6. Take the dough and roll it out thinly, before cutting into 5cm x 7cm rectangles
7. Place 1 tsp of jam in the centre of half the rectangles, wet the edges place another rectangle on the top, and seal
8. Place in the air fryer and cook for 10 minutes
9. Allow to cool
10. Take a bowl and combine the icing sugar, coconut oil, lemon juice, and lemon zest
11. Top the pop tarts with the mixing and add sprinkles

Chocolate Eclairs

Servings - 9
Calories - 200, protein - 2g, fat -11g, carbs - 15g

Ingredients

- 3 eggs
- 150ml/0.6 cups of whipped cream, plus an extra 1 tbsp
- 50g/1.7oz milk chocolate
- 100g/3.5oz plain flour
- 50g/1.7oz butter, plus an extra 25g/0.8oz
- 150ml/0.6 cups of water
- 1 tsp vanilla extract
- 1 tsp icing sugar

Method

1. Preheat the air fryer to 180C/356F
2. Take a pan and add the butter and water, allowing to melt over a medium heat
3. Remove from the heat and stir in the flour slowly
4. Return to the heat until the mix forms a single ball of dough
5. Allow to cool and then beat in the eggs until you have a smooth dough
6. Use your hands to form eclair shapes
7. Cook in the air fryer for 10 minutes and then 160C/320F for 8 minutes
8. Take another bowl and add the vanilla, icing sugar, and whipping cream until thick
9. Once cooled, fill each eclair with the cream mixture
10. Place the chocolate, 1 tbsp whipped cream, and 25g of butter in a glass bowl and melt over a pan of boiling water
11. Top the eclairs with the mixture and allow to set

Banana & Peanut Butter Bites

Servings - 12
Calories - 396, protein - 20g, fat - 21g, carbs - 24g

Ingredients

- 1-2 tsp vegetable oil
- 1 banana, sliced lengthways
- 12 wonton wrappers
- 75g/2.6oz peanut butter

Method

1. Preheat the air fryer to 190C/374F and spray with a little oil
2. Take a wonton wrapper and add one piece of banana and a spoonful of peanut butter inside
3. Wet the edges of each wrapper and fold over to seal
4. Place in the air fryer and cook for 6 minutes

Pistachio & Pecan Brownies

Servings - 4
Calories - 416, protein - 21g, fat - 24g, carbs - 20g

Ingredients

- 75g/2.5oz flour
- 75g/2.6oz sugar
- 25g/0.8oz cocoa powder
- 75ml/0.3 cups of milk
- ½ tsp vanilla extract
- 25g/0.8oz salt
- 25g/0.8oz pecans
- 1 tbsp ground flax seeds

Method

1. Mix all of the dry ingredients together
2. In a separate bowl, mix the wet ingredients
3. Combine both bowls until smooth
4. Preheat the air fryer to 175C/347F
5. Line a 5-inch cake tin with parchment paper
6. Transfer the brownie mixture into the cake tin
7. Cook for about 20 minutes

Joseph Biggs

Fruity Nutella Sandwich

Servings - 2
Calories - 226, protein - 17g, fat - 20g, carbs - 12g

Ingredients
- 1 banana
- 2 tbsp softened butter
- 4 slices white bread
- 25g/0.8oz chocolate spread (Nutella)

Method
1. Preheat your air fryer to 185C/365F
2. Take the bread and spread the butter on one side of each slice
3. Repeat the process with the chocolate spread, using the opposite side of each slice
4. Add sliced banana to two slices of bread then add the other slice of bread to each
5. Cut in half diagonally to form triangles
6. Place in the air fryer and cook for 5 minutes
7. Turn over and cook for another 2 minutes

Peach Pies

Servings - 8
Calories - 406, protein - 21g, fat - 28g, carbs - 23g

Ingredients
- 1 packet of shortcrust pastry
- 2 peaches, chopped
- 1 tsp cornstarch
- 1 tbsp lemon juice
- 3 tbsp sugar
- 1 tsp vanilla extract
- ¼ tsp salt

Method
1. Take a bowl and combine the lemon juice, peaches, sugar, vanilla and salt
2. Allow to rest for 15 minutes
3. Preheat the air fryer to 180C/356F
4. Drain the peaches, retaining 1 tbsp of the juice
5. Mix the liquid with the cornstarch and mix into the peaches
6. Cut out 8x4 inch circles from the pastry
7. Add 1 tbsp of peach mix to each piece of pastry, keeping it to the centre
8. Fold the dough over to create half-moons and crimp the edges with a fork to seal
9. Spray with cooking spray
10. Place in the air fryer and cook for 12-14 minutes

Air Fryer Side Recipes

Whether you're cooking for a special occasion or you want to spruce up dinner a little, these air fryer side recipes will add a little something extra to your lunch or dinner. Many of these side recipes also double up as snacks too!

Spicy Rice

Servings - 4
Calories - 286, protein - 13g, fat - 11g, carbs - 12g

Ingredients

- 3 tbsp olive oil
- 500ml/2 cups of chicken stock
- 500g/17oz long grain rice
- 60ml.02 cups of water
- 1 tsp chilli powder
- 1/4 tsp cumin
- 2 tbsp tomato paste
- 1/2 tsp garlic powder
- 1 tsp red pepper flakes
- 1 onion, chopped
- Half a small jalapeño pepper, de-seeded and chopped
- Salt for seasoning

Method

1. Add a small bowl and add the water and tomato paste. Combine and place to one side
2. Take a baking pan and add a little oil
3. Wash the rice and add to the baking pan
4. Preheat the air fryer to 220C/428F
5. Add the chicken stock, tomato paste, jalapeños, onions, and the rest of the olive oil
6. Combine well and cover with tin foil
7. Place inside the air fryer and cook for 50 minutes

Avocado "Chips"

Servings - 2
Calories - 320, protein - 9g, fat - 18g, carbs - 39g

Ingredients

- 100g/3.5oz panko breadcrumbs
- 1 ripe avocado, cut into 8 slices
- 150g/5.2oz flour
- ½ tsp black pepper
- ¼ tsp salt
- 1 egg
- 1 tsp water

Method

1. Preheat the air fryer to 200C/392F
2. Take a bowl and combine the flour, salt and pepper
3. Beat the egg and water together in another bowl
4. Add the breadcrumbs to a third bowl
5. Dip the avocado into the flour, then the egg, then into the breadcrumbs
6. Spray with cooking oil and place in the air fryer
7. Cook for 4 minutes
8. Turn the avocado and cook for a further 3 minutes

Parmesan Asparagus

Servings - 4
Calories - 296, protein - 11g, fat - 3g, carbs - 12g

Ingredients

- 1 tsp olive oil
- 1 tbsp grated parmesan cheese
- 500g/17oz asparagus
- 1 tsp garlic salt
- Salt and pepper for seasoning

Method

1. Preheat your air fryer to 270C/518F
2. Clean the asparagus and cut off the bottom section
3. Pat dry and place in the air fryer, covering with the oil
4. Sprinkle the parmesan and garlic salt on top
5. Season to your liking
6. Cook for 10 minutes
7. Sprinkle with extra parmesan before serving

Balsamic Brussels

Servings - 2
Calories - 100, protein - 5g, fat - 9g, carbs -13g

Ingredients
- 400g/14oz Brussels sprouts, halved
- 1 tsp balsamic vinegar
- 2 tsp cooked bacon, crumbled
- 1 tbsp avocado oil
- ½ tsp salt
- ½ tsp pepper

Method
1. Preheat your air fryer to 175C/347F
2. Take a bowl and combine the oil, salt, and pepper
3. Add the Brussels sprouts and coat well
4. Place in the air fryer and cook for 5 minutes
5. Shake and cook for another 5 minutes
6. Sprinkle with balsamic vinegar and bacon before serving

Corn on The Cob

Servings - 4
Calories - 196, protein - 11g, fat - 15g, carbs - 21g

Ingredients

- 2 ears of corn, cut into 4 pieces
- 75g/2.6oz mayonnaise
- 2 tsp grated cheese
- 1 tsp lime juice
- ¼ tsp chilli powder

Method

1. Heat your air fryer to 200C/392F
2. Mix the mayonnaise, cheese, lime juice, and chilli powder in a bowl
3. Cover the corn in the mayonnaise mix, ensuring it is totally coated
4. Place in the air fryer and cook for 8 minutes

Herby Baby Potatoes

Servings - 4
Calories - 100, protein - 2g, fat - 0.3g, carbs - 20g

Ingredients

- 500g/17oz baby potatoes, quartered
- 1 tbsp oil
- ½ tsp garlic powder
- ½ tsp dried parsley
- 1 tsp salt

Method

1. Preheat your air fryer to 175C/347F
2. Take a bowl and combine the oil and potatoes
3. Add remaining ingredients and combine again
4. Add to the air fryer
5. Cook for 25 minutes until golden brown. Make sure you turn halfway through

Cheesy Shishito Peppers

Servings - 2
Calories - 256, protein - 2.5g, fat - 3g, carbs - 2g

Ingredients
- ½ tbsp avocado oil
- 200g/7oz shishito peppers
- 75g/2.6oz grated cheese
- 2 limes
- Salt and pepper to taste

Method
1. Preheat your air fryer to 175C/347F
2. Place the peppers into a bowl and mix with the oil, salt, and pepper
3. Place in the air fryer and cook for 10 minutes
4. Sprinkle with cheese before serving

Mini Aubergine (Eggplant) Bites

Servings - 4
Calories - 200, protein - 21g, fat - 26g, carbs - 21g

Ingredients
- 100g/3.5oz flour
- 2 eggs
- 1 aubergine/eggplant, sliced into ½ inch rounds
- 100g/3.5oz Italian breadcrumbs
- 50g/1.7oz grated parmesan
- 1 tsp Italian seasoning
- 1 tsp salt
- ½ tsp dried basil
- ½ tsp onion powder
- ½ tsp black pepper

Method
1. Preheat the air fryer to 185C/365F
2. Take a bowl and combine the breadcrumbs, parmesan, salt, Italian seasoning, basil, onion powder, and pepper
3. Add the flour to another bowl, and beat the eggs in another
4. Dip the aubergine/eggplant in the flour, then the eggs, and then coat in the breadcrumbs
5. Place the aubergine in the air fryer and cook for 8 minutes
6. Turnover and cook for a further 4 minutes

Cheesy Carrot Fries

Servings - 2
Calories - 126, protein - 27g, fat - 22g, carbs - 24g

Ingredients

- 1 tbsp olive oil
- 180g/6.3oz carrots, halved
- 1 garlic clove, crushed
- 2 tbsp parmesan, grated
- Salt and pepper for seasoning

Method

1. Preheat your air fryer to 220C/428F
2. Combine the olive oil and garlic in a bowl
3. Add the carrots to the bowl and combine again
4. Add the parmesan and make sure everything is coated in the mixture
5. Add the carrots to the air fryer and cook for 20 minutes, shaking halfway through

Spinach Stuffed Potatoes

Servings - 4
Calories - 416, protein - 26g, fat - 23g, carbs - 28g

Ingredients
- 2 large potatoes
- 50g/1.7oz spinach, chopped
- 2 tbsp nutritional yeast
- 2 tsp olive oil
- 100ml/0.5 cups of milk
- 100ml/0.5 cups of yogurt
- ¼ tsp pepper
- ½ tsp salt

Method
1. Preheat the air fryer to 190C/374F
2. Rub the potatoes with oil and place in the air fryer
3. Cook for 30 minutes, turn and cook for another 30 minutes
4. Once cooked, cut the potatoes in half and remove the middles with a spoon
5. Mash the potato with the milk, yeast, and yogurt
6. Add the spinach, seasoning, and combine again
7. Spoon the mixture back inside the skins and return to the air fryer
8. Cook at 160C/320F for 5 minutes

Citrus & Garlic Tofu

Servings - 4
Calories -100, protein - 6g, fat - 10g, carbs - 10g

Ingredients

- 400g/14oz tofu, drained and cubed
- 2 tsp cornstarch
- 1 tbsp maple syrup
- 1 tsp orange zest
- 75ml/0.3 cups of orange juice
- 1 tbsp tamari
- 1 tbsp corn starch
- ¼ tsp pepper flakes
- 1 tsp minced ginger
- 1 tsp fresh garlic
- 75ml/0.3 cups of water

Method

1. Place the tofu in a bowl with the tamari and combine
2. Mix in 1 tbsp cornstarch and rest for 30 minutes
3. Preheat your air fryer to 190C/374F
4. Place the remaining ingredients into another bowl and combine
5. Place the tofu in the air fryer and cook for about 10 minutes
6. Add tofu to a pan with sauce the mix and cook until sauce begins to thicken

Courgette (Zucchini) Gratin

Servings - 2
Calories - 183, protein - 13g, fat - 16g, carbs - 2g

Ingredients
- 2 courgettes/zucchinis
- 1 tbsp vegetable oil
- 1 tbsp parsley, chopped
- 4 tbsp parmesan, grated
- 2 tbsp breadcrumbs
- Salt and pepper to taste

Method
1. Heat yo ur air fryer to 180/356F
2. Cut each courgette in half lengthways and then cut into slices
3. Mix the remaining ingredients together in a bowl
4. Place the courgette in the air fryer and top with the breadcrumb mixture
5. Cook for 15 minutes

Salty Chickpeas

Servings - 5
Calories - 230, protein - 6g, fat - 8g, carbs - 30g

Ingredients

- 1 tbsp olive oil
- 1 can of chickpeas, drained
- 100ml/0.5 cups of white vinegar
- Salt to taste

Method

1. Take a pan and combine the chickpeas and vinegar over a medium heat
2. Allow to simmer, remove from the heat and rest for 30 minutes
3. Preheat the air fryer to 190C/374F
4. Place the chickpeas into the air fryer and cook for 4 minutes
5. Once cooked, pour the chickpeas into an ovenproof bowl
6. Drizzle with the oil and season
7. Place the bowl into the air fryer and cook for another 4 minutes

Spicy Pickles

Servings - 4
Calories - 170, protein - 2g, fat - 16g, carbs - 15g

Ingredients
- 1 jar of dill pickle slices
- 1 egg
- 2 tbsp milk
- 50g/1.7oz flour
- 118ml/0.5 cups of mayonnaise
- 2 tsp sriracha sauce
- 50g/1.7oz cornmeal
- ½ tsp seasoned salt
- ¼ tsp paprika
- ¼ tsp garlic powder
- ⅛ tsp pepper
- Cooking spray

Method
1. Mix the mayonnaise and sriracha together in a bowl and set aside
2. Preheat the air fryer to 200C/392F
3. Drain the pickles and pat dry
4. Mix the egg and milk together
5. In another bowl, mix all the remaining ingredients together
6. Dip the pickles into the egg mixture and then into the flour mixture
7. Spray the air fryer with cooking spray and place the pickles inside the basket
8. Cook for about 4 minutes, until crispy

BBQ Bacon Parcels

Servings - 4
Calories - 250, protein - 20g, fat - 30g, carbs - 20g

Ingredients
- 2 chicken breasts
- 7 slices of bacon, cut lengthwise and then into halves
- 200ml/0.8 cups of BBQ sauce
- 2 tbsp brown sugar

Method
1. Preheat the air fryer to 220C/428F
2. Take a piece of chicken and wrap two strips of the bacon around it
3. Brush with the BBQ sauce and sprinkle with the brown sugar
4. Repeat with the rest of the chicken and bacon
5. Place the parcels into the air fryer basket and cook for 5 minutes
6. Turn the chicken over and cook for another 5 minutes

Conclusion

By this point, you should be totally convinced that purchasing an air fryer is for you. If you already have one and it's been pushed into the back of the kitchen cupboard, barely seeing the light of day, now is the time to grab it and let it shine!

You should be feeling ready to start creating delicious recipes using your new appliance. You're probably spoiled for choice and don't know which one to choose first!

You can make all of these recipes very easily with your air fryer, and the other good news is that all the ingredients we've mentioned can be found in your local supermarket or grocery store, no issues at all! So, you have no excuses not to get started, today!

By choosing to embrace your air fryer, you'll find that cooking for yourself is a much healthier and cost effective way to live. You know exactly what has gone into your food, there are no added nasties, and you're saving money because we all know that takeaways are expensive. By cooking for yourself you can source the most delicious and fresh produce to put into your recipes, and you're getting the maximum nutritional value possible.

Your health is vital. You can easily make choices that impact detrimentally on your health but you can also make choices that have a positive effect too. Choosing an air fryer and working with it as much as possible will help you to become healthier, give a new hobby (cooking for yourself), will save you money, and will show you just how delicious food can be when it's truly fresh.

The fact that you're not cooking in oil is a huge nod towards health and if you're someone who does that crisp you get from your food, the air fryer will do that for you too!

So, which recipe will you choose first? You can go in there and look at what you fancy the most, or you can simply click at random and then vow to make that particular recipe. Don't be afraid to try new things, either. Maybe we've mentioned a recipe with an ingredient you've never tried before. Just give it a go! Who knows, you might like it! You might discover something new you like as well as discover your air fryer too.

Remember that practice makes perfect and the more you use your new appliance, the more you'll feel able to keep pushing your limits and trying new things. Your confidence will grow as you use your air fryer more and more. Your nearest and dearest will also thank you for your new choice, as their meals will be healthier and more flavourful too!

So, grab your air fryer and become acquainted with it. Then, choose your first recipe and get started. Once you go air fryer, you'll never go back!

EXCLUSIVE BONUS

40 Weight Loss Recipes

&

14 Days Meal Plan

Scan the QR-Code and receive the FREE download:

Disclaimer

This book contains opinions and ideas of the author and is meant to teach the reader informative and helpful knowledge while due care should be taken by the user in the application of the information provided. The instructions and strategies are possibly not right for every reader and there is no guarantee that they work for everyone. Using this book and implementing the information/recipes therein contained is explicitly your own responsibility and risk. This work with all its contents, does not guarantee correctness, completion, quality or correctness of the provided information. Misinformation or misprints cannot be completely eliminated.

Printed in Great Britain
by Amazon